پنچان قیصہ نبی علیہم السّلام

Ismail and Ya'qub

Abdul Rahman Rukaini

M

MACMILLAN PUBLISHERS

Bahasa Malay edition first published 1984.
Published by Macmillan Publishers (M) Sdn. Bhd. co-publication with
Pustaka Pertubuhan Kebajikan Islam Malaysia.

This edition first published 1985

Published by *Macmillan Publishers Ltd*
London and Basingstoke
Associated companies and representatives in Accra,
Auckland, Delhi, Dublin, Gaborone, Hamburg, Harare,
Hong Kong, Kuala Lumpur, Lagos, Manzini, Melbourne,
Mexico City, Nairobi, New York, Singapore, Tokyo

ISBN 0−333−41419−5 (cased)
ISBN 0−333−40017−8 (pbk)

Printed in Hong Kong

Adviser for text:
Ustaz Haji Abu Hassan Din al-Hafiz

Adviser for illustrations:
Abdul Aziz Ibrahim

Designer and artist:
Abdul Razak Abdullah
(ERAL)

*Illustrations found in these series were not meant to
depict all the prophets, their companions, or anyone
concerned during that time. These illustrations were
only meant to picture the situation or episodes that
happened during that time. The Publisher has
consulted authorised personnel to seek their advice
regarding the contents and illustrations.*

British Library Cataloguing in Publication Data
Rukaini, Abdul Rahman
   Stories of the prophets of Islam.
   1. Prophets in the Koran—Biography—Juvenile
   literature
   I. Title
   297′.122′0922   BP134.P745

ISBN 0−333−41419−5 (cased)
ISBN 0−333−40017−8 (pbk)

Preface

This volume tells the story of how the prophet Ibrahim travelled to the desert of the Arabian peninsula with Hajar and his infant son, Ismail. His departure from his first wife, Sarah, and later his departure from Hajar and Ismail, show just how patiently and calmly the prophet Ibrahim carried out the command of Allah.

In this volume we also learn of the prophet Ismail and the prophet Ya'qub. The story of the prophet Ismail, is an important one because it is one on which the performance of the Haj is based.

The stories were carefully selected and creatively written to capture the interest of young readers.

Illustrations

Contents

Hajar the true-hearted

Hajar was a slave, chosen by the prophet Ibrahim to help his wife, Sarah, in the house. She worked hard and did everything well. Wherever Ibrahim and Sarah went, she went with them, and never failed in her duty to her master.

The people of Babylon, Palestine and Egypt all spoke well of her. 'Hajar is the most faithful of slaves', they said. 'She is unique. She is hard-working, beautiful and charming. Hajar has a good heart.'

Near Ibrahim's home in Palestine a man was talking to his wife.

'I don't like Ibrahim', he said, looking in the direction of Ibrahim's house but thinking of Hajar.

His wife remained silent. She had nothing against Ibrahim but she was

too afraid to argue with her husband.

'But I'm very impressed with Hajar', he continued, smiling to himself.

'I know what you mean', agreed his wife. She didn't want to start an argument.

'I'm glad you understand', said her husband, still gazing out of the window. 'Hajar is clever, hard-working and honest. It's a shame she is only a slave.' He sighed as if he longed to be able to change Hajar's position.

His wife agreed that Hajar was efficient and honest but she knew what good people Ibrahim and Sarah were and she had to speak out. 'Ibrahim and Sarah don't treat her like a slave. They work hard too. They don't just give commands.'

'That's what you think', said her husband, unconvinced.

'It's not just what I think. Everyone says that. Everyone knows it's true.' She didn't want to annoy him, and looking out of the window she said, 'Look, you can see Hajar's footprints in the sand. She's going to fetch water, even though the sun is so high in the sky.'

The man was annoyed he had missed seeing Hajar pass by. 'Beautiful, beautiful', he murmured, stroking his beard and gazing at her footprints, 'Such a pity she's a slave.'

'She's a lucky slave, though', objected his wife. She thought she knew what her husband was thinking.

'A lucky slave?' asked the man, surprised.

'Yes, she is lucky, and everyone knows it!' said his wife.

'I don't understand you', said the man, beginning to suspect there was something he didn't know.

His wife smiled at his words but she said nothing.

'You're laughing at me', said her husband, growing angry.

'I see you truly haven't heard', his wife replied calmly. 'Hajar is not just any woman. She does not need the pity of people like us. She has a good life with Ibrahim and Sarah. Sarah has suggested to Ibrahim that he marry Hajar.'

'No, I don't believe it!' her husband shouted. He would not listen to her any more and he left the house with a feeling of pain and loss as he followed Hajar's footprints in the sand.

The prophet takes a wife

Since hearing about Sarah's suggestion that Ibrahim should marry Hajar, the man had changed. He was quiet and thoughtful. A war was raging in his heart between hope and resignation as he tried to accept the truth.

His wife accepted the change in him calmly. She understood what he was feeling.

'How do you know this?' he asked her one evening as the sun was setting.

'About Ibrahim marrying Hajar?'

asked his wife. 'I heard it from someone who often goes to Ibrahim's house. Someone who never tells lies', she added firmly. She wanted him to forget his desires so there could be harmony between them again.

'Ibrahim and Sarah have been married a long time', she began, as her husband continued to gaze at the setting sun. 'They are getting old – but they don't have a child.'

'A child?' asked her husband. He sounded surprised that the couple should want a child.

'Yes, Ibrahim and Sarah want a child,' his wife continued earnestly, 'but Sarah could not have a child.'

Her husband was silent. He wasn't very interested in the subject of children.

'So, because they wanted a child,' his wife continued, 'Sarah suggested to Ibrahim that he should marry Hajar.'

'But surely Ibrahim would not marry his slave?' her husband cried.

'Hajar's goodness makes her as worthy as Sarah', said his wife.

'And Ibrahim agreed?'

'He refused at first. He loved Sarah even though she could not have a child. He asked Sarah to think carefully about her suggestion', his wife explained.

The husband began to feel himself unworthy in comparison with Ibrahim's goodness.

'Did he really?' he asked.

'Yes, he did not want Sarah to regret it later', said his wife.

Ibrahim is a good man, thought the man to himself, but he did not say it aloud. His wife told him how Ibrahim had still hoped that one day Allah would give Sarah a child, but Sarah knew that was just a dream. She was too old, and she urged Ibrahim to marry Hajar. Sarah had to persuade Hajar too. In the end everyone agreed and Ibrahim and Hajar married.

'Now Hajar is a slave no longer', said the man. He was deeply moved by the story of these three good, honest people, and he had learned from it. Turning to his wife he told her that he now recognised that Ibrahim was indeed the prophet of Allah.

When the time came, Hajar gave birth to a baby boy. He was named Ismail. The prophet Ibrahim was overjoyed to have a son and he wanted to share his happiness with Sarah. But Sarah could not hide her sadness and she could not accept the child even though Ibrahim had said it was a gift from Allah.

Where could they have gone?

'So the prophet Ibrahim and Hajar left Palestine!' said the woman's husband sorrowfully.

'Yes, they left', explained his wife. 'It was the will of Allah that they must leave Palestine.'

The man looked out of the window at the goats which now wandered aimlessly, and the wilted crops that no one tended. It had always been Hajar who led the goats through the desert in search of grass, Hajar who fetched water for the crops. The earth of Palestine seemed to be mourning for Hajar's footsteps.

'Where have they gone?' asked the man.

'They headed south,' his wife replied, 'but no one knows where they are now.'

The man rose. He looked out of the window, his gaze searching the dunes of the desert in the distance. He imagined the hardships which even now Ibrahim, Hajar and Ismail might be enduring.

'How did they go?' he asked.

'By camel', replied his wife. 'How else?'

Husband and wife stood side by side, wondering where Ibrahim, his wife and baby had gone, to what land they had made their way. All they knew was that Ibrahim would trust in Allah.

Their lips moved silently as they prayed for the well-being of Ibrahim, Ismail and Hajar. The question in their minds remained unanswered. Where could they have gone?

Don't leave us!

بِسْمِ اللهِ الرَّحْمٰنِ الرَّحِيمِ

The land of Palestine was silent, as if it felt a loss. Black clouds covered the sky, as if in mourning. Even the gentle breeze seemed to be searching for the faces of the prophet Ibrahim, Ismail and Hajar.

But they had left the land of Palestine. They had left Sarah with her sorrow. With heavy hearts they journeyed on. They went where the camels took them. Ismail was just a baby but he seemed to understand and did not cry. There was no complaint from Hajar either. She accepted all that happened as the will of Allah. The prophet Ibrahim, too, believed this journey to nowhere had been decided by Allah, and asked His protection for himself, his wife and his child.

In the heat of the day and the dark of the night, the little group wandered in a sea of sand. At last, after weeks of journeying, the camels stopped in a valley between two hills. That valley was Makkah. There was nothing there but sand, stones and the bare hills.

The prophet Ibrahim got down from his camel. Hajar got down too, with Ismail. Anxiety swelled in Hajar's breast. There was nothing here. Surely she and her child would suffer hunger and thirst?

Ibrahim looked at Ismail's innocent face, then at Hajar. His heart sank at the thought of what he must do. Allah had ordered that he should leave them here and return to Palestine alone. When he told Hajar of Allah's command, she wept with sorrow. She pleaded with the prophet Ibrahim to have pity on herself and the child.

'Who will protect us if you go?' she asked him, as tears ran down her cheeks. 'How can you bear to part with your child?' Hajar clung to the hem of his robe. She was terrified at the thought of their separation. 'Don't leave us, please . . .' she begged.

He was torn at the sight of her sadness. 'If it were not commanded by Allah, I would never leave you here with the child', he told her. 'Have faith Hajar, Allah the Almighty will not allow you to suffer harm. His blessings and protection will always be with you.'

Slowly Hajar let go of the hem of Ibrahim's robe. She tried to find courage in her faith in Allah and confidence in His blessings.

They both wept at the thought of their separation. They did not know if they would meet again.

The prophet Ibrahim walked slowly away. Then he stopped for a moment. He lifted his hands and prayed, 'O My God, I place my child and the children of his descent in this dry and barren valley, near Your house (*Baitullah*), so that they may worship You and follow Your law. Let the hearts of men take pity on them and give them sweet fruits to eat, that they may bless You . . .' (*Al Quran, Surah Ibrahim, verse 37*)

When he had finished his prayer, the prophet Ibrahim got on his camel and rode away, leaving Hajar and his small child, Ismail, alone.

Water! Water!

A group of travellers were camping in a barren valley on their way to Makkah. They were very thirsty and knew there was no water nearby. Then, to their surprise, one of the travellers held up his water-jar and shouted, 'Water! Water!' He passed

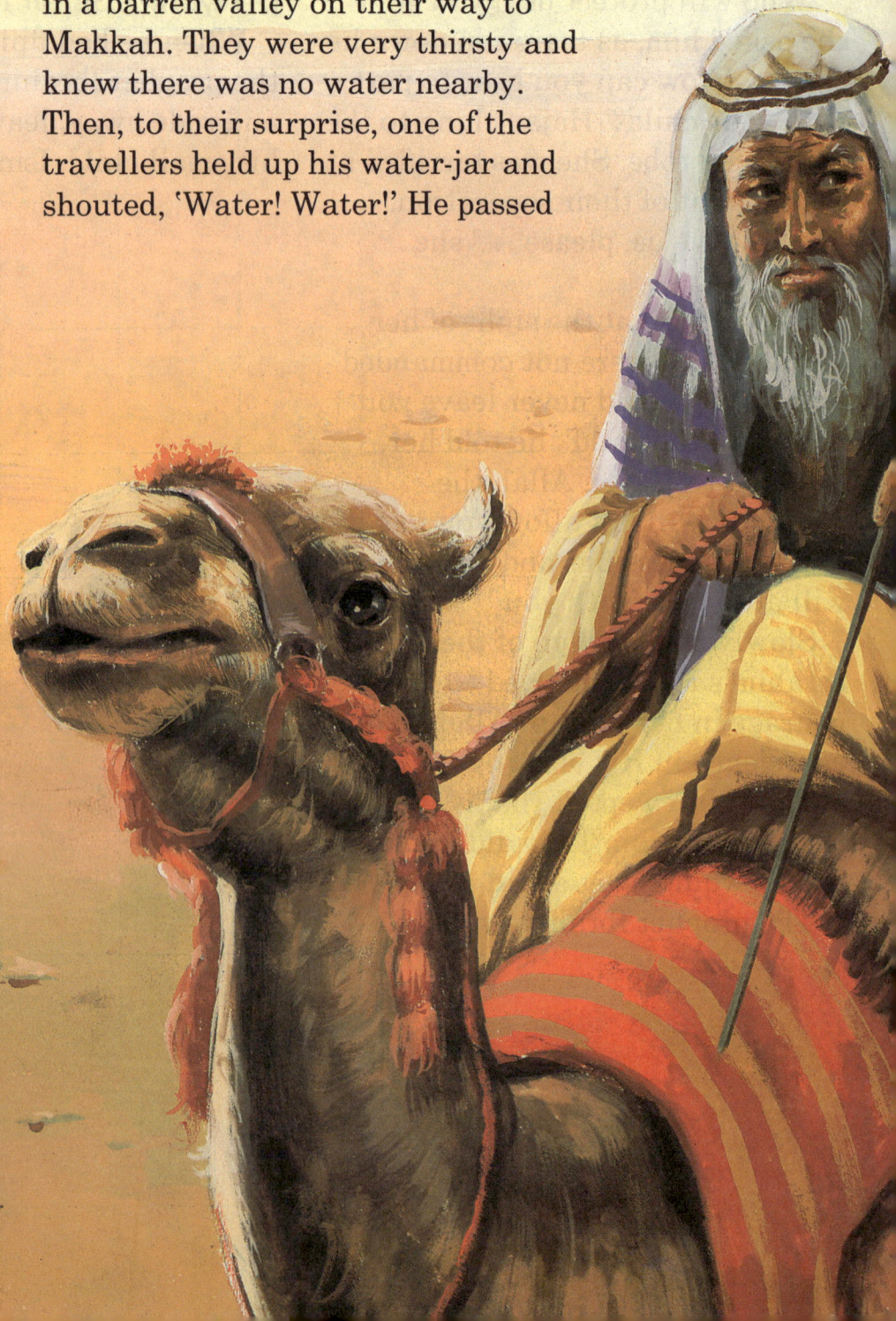

the jar round and everyone drank thankfully.

'Where did you get this water from?' asked one of the men.

'From the Zam-zam well', he replied. The people were astonished at the strange name of the well.

'It's between the two hills: the hills of Safa and Marwa', explained the man.

'I've never seen a well there', said one of the travellers.

'How could there be a well there?' said another. 'No one lives there.'

'There is a well there, and there are people there', replied the man.

The others were astonished. They did not think anyone could live in such a place.

'A mother and her child live

there', continued the man. 'The woman is not just any woman. She has great faith in Allah. She is good and patient. Her name is Hajar and her son's name is Ismail.' The man had known of Hajar and Ismail in Palestine. 'She is the wife of a prophet called Ibrahim', he added.

'Did he leave the mother and child there, without shelter or water?' asked one of the people. They all wanted to know more about Hajar and Ismail, so the man told them what had happened when Ibrahim rode away:

Soon Hajar had no food and water left, and no one passed by. She was hungry and thirsty but Ibrahim had told her it was Allah's will she should be left there, and she bore the burning sun and the loneliness with patience. Ismail suffered too. When he began to cry, Hajar tried to comfort him but she could not help him. She searched and searched for water until she could hardly stand. Then Hajar thought she heard someone call her name. She ran between the hills of Safa and Marwa, but there was no one there. She was in despair.

Ismail was crying more and more, his heels stamping the ground. Hajar prayed for Allah's protection and Allah sent the angel Jibril.

Then Hajar saw water springing from a crack in the ground beneath Ismail's heel. She could hardly believe her eyes. She dug at the sand around the spring. She cupped the water in her hands and, lifting it carefully, let Ismail drink. He was quiet now and Hajar was no longer afraid.

'The water continued to flow until it became a well', said the man.

'So the water we drank came from that well?' asked the travellers.

'Yes', said the man. 'It was water from the Zam-zam well; a well created from sorrow, patience, and a mother's faith in Allah.'

'The Zam-zam well! Water! Water from the Zam-zam well!' the people cried together. They rejoiced as they left their camp and continued on their way to Makkah.

The plain of Arafah

Many years had passed since Ibrahim had left Hajar and Ismail in the barren valley. He prayed for them every day and the more he prayed, the more he missed them. His heart ached when he remembered Hajar's cry, 'Don't leave us! Don't leave us!' He worried about what had happened to them, but he had faith in Allah. It was Allah who had commanded that it should be done. Allah would bring them ease or suffering, life or death ...

Ibrahim would eagerly question the travellers who had passed through the barren valley on the way to Palestine. The good news they brought made him long to see his wife and child again. When he told Sarah, she immediately said, 'Then you must go.' She understood her husband's needs.

So once again Ibrahim went south,

across the vast desert. But this time he knew where he was going. He prayed to Allah to bless this journey and give him His protection.

Palestine was far behind, but when Ibrahim saw a caravan of traders coming from the valley he wondered if he had come to the right place. People were camping in the foothills, and fetching water.

'Can this be the place where I left Hajar and my son Ismail?' Ibrahim asked himself. He got down from his camel and went towards a group of people who were carrying water containers. He wondered where they could be going to get water from in this barren valley. When Ibrahim asked the people about Hajar and Ismail, they showed him the well. It belonged to Hajar and Ismail, they said. The water had sprung from the ground beneath Ismail's heel. When Ibrahim heard this, he gave praise to Allah. Allah had granted his prayers.

Ibrahim smiled as he walked towards the camp to find Hajar and Ismail. His heart was full of joy at the thought of seeing them again.

But Hajar and Ismail were not at the camp. They were looking after their goats in the fields, someone told him, and showed him the way.

Ibrahim got on his camel again and set off for the fields, which were outside Makkah. At last he came to the place which is known as the field of Arafah ('the place of meeting and friendship'). A woman and a boy were patiently tending their goats. The prophet Ibrahim knew at once that the woman was Hajar, his wife, and the boy was his son, Ismail.

Hajar looked up and saw him. She jumped up in joy and, taking the child by the hand, ran towards him. Ibrahim embraced his wife and child. Tears of joy ran down their cheeks as they said prayers of thanks to Allah:

Allaahu Akbar!
(Allah is the Greatest!)
Allaahu Akbar!
(Allah is the Greatest!)
Allaahu Akbar!
(Allah is the Greatest!)
Wali'llahi'l-Hamd!
(And all praise to Allah!)

The sacrifice

As the sun began to set, the prophet Ibrahim, Hajar and Ismail left the field of Arafah and made their way towards Makkah. The burning heat of the day slowly changed to the cool of night as shadows fell over the

desert. It was late, so they stopped for the night at Muzdalifah.

While he slept, the prophet Ibrahim dreamt that Allah commanded him to sacrifice his beloved son, Ismail. He woke with a start and looked at Ismail asleep nearby. As he looked at the boy's face, he understood that his dream really was a command from Allah.

The next morning they woke and prayed to Allah. Then Ibrahim put his hands on Ismail's shoulders and gazed into his eyes. The boy's eyes shone with love for the father he had missed for so long. Ibrahim found it difficult to speak. 'I had a dream last night,' he said softly. 'It makes me very sad to tell you about it.'

'Please tell me, father. I am ready to hear', said Ismail calmly. Ismail's words helped Ibrahim face his duty to carry out the will of Allah.

'Oh, my son, I dreamt that Allah commanded me to sacrifice you', said the prophet.

When he heard his father's words, Ismail said calmly, 'Father, carry out Allah's command. I have the courage to obey His will.' (*Al Quran, Surah al-Saffat, verse 102*) Ismail already showed the great faith and loyalty to Allah of a future prophet and messenger of Allah. This was not the first test which Ibrahim and his family had faced. Ibrahim would obey Allah's command because his loyalty to Allah was even stronger than his great love for his son.

The prophet Ibrahim and his son set out for the Hill of Angels, in Mina. This was where they would carry out Allah's command for the greatest of sacrifices – the sacrifice of a human life. Their courage and their faith were so great that they did not hesitate once.

At a crossroads they met a man who asked them where they were going. When the prophet Ibrahim explained, the man tried to dissuade them.

'Do not kill your only son', he said. 'Just think how long you waited for him and how you nearly lost him. His life cannot be replaced.'

But the man's words did not make Ibrahim and Ismail doubt what they had to do. They knew that this man was Iblis, hoping to tempt them. They picked up stones and threw them at the man until he fell to the ground. Then they left the place, which is now called Jamrah al-Ula, and went on their way.

As they walked on, they met another man who tried to persuade them to forget Allah's command. Again they ignored his words, and stoned him to the ground. That man was also Iblis in disguise and the place is now called Jamrah al-Wusta. It is 156 metres from Jamrah al-Ula.

They walked on and they were tempted a third time by another man who was really Iblis in disguise. This was at the place now known as Jamrah al-Aqabah, which is about 156 metres from Jamrah al-Wusta, and they stoned this man too.

At last they arrived at the foot of the Hill of Angels at Mina. They got ready to carry out the sacrifice.

'Now, father, you must carry out Allah's command', said Ismail. 'I will obey anything you say. But first, may I ask something of you? Please tie me tightly so I won't move and make it difficult for you. Take off my clothes, then my blood won't stain them and grieve my mother when she sees it. Sharpen your sword and kill me quickly so I do not suffer too much. Remember me to my mother and give her my clothes. They may comfort her in her grief, as a remembrance of her only son.'

The prophet Ibrahim was deeply moved by his son's brave words. He embraced him and kissed him.

'Allah has blessed me with a son who is loyal, repectful and has the goodness in his heart to obey Allah's will without hesitation.'

Ibrahim gripped his sharpened sword in his hand. Ismail lay in front of him, tightly bound. They said their farewells and prayed to Allah. Then, as the prophet put the point of his sword to Ismail's throat, he heard a voice from the hilltop.

Ibrahim turned round and saw a healthy and fat sheep. The voice continued,

'Ibrahim, take this sheep in place of Ismail', said the voice. 'Kill the sheep and eat its meat. This shall be a day of celebration for you. Give some of the meat to the poor as part of your sacrifice.' The angel left the sheep and disappeared.

The prophet Ibrahim killed the sheep. Its blood soaked into the earth. Ibrahim and Ismail ate some of the meat and gave the rest to others.

With this sacrifice of the sheep, Allah saved Ismail and blessed the family of Ibrahim. The Celebration Day of the Sacrifice, when Muslims all over the world kill a sheep even today, is in memory of Ibrahim and Ismail's sacrifice of the sheep. The things we do during the Haj follow the things that were done by Hajar, the prophet Ibrahim, and their son, Ismail.

Prayer in the Ka'abah

Although Ibrahim knew that Hajar and Ismail were well and happy, he still felt very sad when he was not with them. He prayed to Allah all the time that he might be able to see them again.

At last Allah sent him a command in a dream and once more the prophet Ibrahim set off on the long, difficult journey to Makkah. But the hardships of the journey meant nothing to him as he thought of his dream. Allah had commanded him to build the 'house of Allah' or the Ka'abah. He longed to reach Makkah.

As soon as he arrived in Makkah Ibrahim got off his camel and went to meet Ismail at the Zam-zam well. Somehow he knew that was where Ismail would be. Ismail greeted the prophet Ibrahim with respect. He had not seen his father for a long time but his love was just as great.

The prophet Ibrahim told his son of his dream. 'Allah has commanded me to build a house on high ground here', he said, pointing in the direction of the high ground near the Zam-zam well.

Ismail was delighted. Allah had

spoken. They began work at once.

In the dream, Jibril had told Ibrahim how to build the Ka'abah. Ismail fetched stones from the hills nearby and Ibrahim laid them. They worked from sunrise to sunset and as they worked, the prophet Ibrahim prayed:

'O Allah! Accept our offering.
You the All-hearing
and All-knowing.
O Allah!
Let us remain, Your followers.
And our children
and our children's children,
so they may become
the family of Islam.
Show us the way to worship.
Have mercy on us, for truly
You are the All-forgiving
and Loving.' (*Al Quran, Surah Al Baqara, verses 127–128*)

Ibrahim always said this prayer in a particular place which is now called the Maqam Ibrahim. Here he built a high stone wall. The last stone, which he set in place low down, was a special black stone (the Hajar Aswad). This stone had been carried once round the Ka'abah before it was put in place. Ibrahim and Ismail kissed the stone in praise of Allah now that their work was finished. They were astonished to see that each time they kissed it, the light of Allah's love shone from the stone. This was the love which would surround the family of Islam.

Allah sent the angel Jibril to show Ibrahim and Ismail how to worship. The same ceremonies were still performed in the time of the Prophet Muhammad.

Ibrahim prayed for peace in the land, and food for the people who believed in Allah and the Day of Judgement. He prayed to Allah to send the people a prophet, one of their own people, to teach them wisdom and truth, and purify them. Then the prophet Ibrahim and Ismail joined their voices in a prayer for mankind:

'O Allah!
I have left some of my children to make their home in a barren valley near Your sacred house.
Let them worship You.
Put kindness towards them in men's hearts.
Provide them with fruits of the earth
so they may give thanks to You.'

Then Ibrahim and Ismail brought others to worship at the Ka'abah.

Brotherly love

Many years later, some of Ibrahim's descendants were living in Syria (Kan'an). The prophet Ishaq and his wife, Rifqah, had two sons, Isu and Ya'qub. Isu had two beautiful wives and several children but Ya'qub was

up in surprise at his words. Isu's face was red with anger.

'I hate him. He is the favourite son.' Isu put down the plate of meat he was carrying. The two wives realised the prophet Ishaq had

not married. Isu, though, was not happy.

'I hate him', said Isu, as he came into the room. His two wives looked

refused Isu's food. The first wife asked him why.

'Why do you think? He'd already eaten the food prepared for him by

Ya'qub,' said Isu angrily.

'What did Ishaq say?' asked the second wife.

'He said I should accept it as the will of Allah', replied Isu. 'But that's not all', he continued. 'My father has given his blessing to Ya'qub and prayed that Allah will make Ya'qub's descendants prophets. So I and my descendants are not blessed . . .'

Isu's voice broke off. He was bitterly angry and hated Ya'qub. He decided that Ya'qub was now his enemy and told his wives they must have nothing to do with him. The wives meekly agreed. They did everything Isu told them.

Ya'qub was miserable. He could not understand the behaviour of Isu and his wives. He was never rude to them, though. He tried to win back his brother's love with patience and kindness. But nothing worked. Ya'qub was in despair. He prayed to Allah. He hoped Allah could make Isu accept Allah's will, but nothing changed. Their mother, Rifqah, tried to help but Isu's hatred grew deeper and deeper. In the end Ya'qub tried to avoid seeing Isu. He realised he could not change his brother's mind. So he went to see his father, the prophet Ishaq.

Ya'qub looked very unhappy.

'Father, I've come to ask your advice', he began. The prophet had heard about the family quarrels and listened sympathetically while Ya'qub told him the whole story.

'My own brother hates me', said Ya'qub sadly. 'He has beautiful wives, and children. He is wealthy. I have nothing but he will not talk to me. We are not brothers any more. Father, I have come to ask you if you can do anything about it.'

The prophet Ishaq stroked his beard. 'I am old', he said. 'I should not like to die while there is a quarrel between you and your brother.' He was silent for a moment as he thought. Ya'qub bowed his head and waited.

'My child,' said Ishaq at last, 'I think it would be best if you went to your uncle, Laban bin Batwail, in Iraq. Marry one of his daughters and live there in peace and happiness. Then come back to Syria. May Allah protect you and your descendants. 'I will pray that the quarrel between you and your brother will be forgotten and you will love each other again.'

Ya'qub obeyed his father and got ready to leave Syria.

He left his father, his mother and the brother he still loved, despite Isu's hatred for him.

Crossing the desert

Ya'qub had to cross a desert to reach the land where his uncle lived. The heat of the sun burned his skin and dust covered his feet. As he walked, and when he rested in the shade of rocks and caves, he prayed constantly to Allah for His protection. The memory of his father's words, 'May you live in peace and happiness', gave him the strength to keep going. He was so tired, that once, when he stopped to rest, he fell asleep and dreamed that Allah spoke to him. A voice said:
'I am Allah.
There is no God but Allah.
I am your God and the God of your father.
I have prepared the Holy Land (*Baitul Muqaddis*) for you and your children,
I bless them and I give you wisdom and power.
I make you My prophet.'
Ya'qub woke with a start. His strength returned and he walked on, happy to know that this long and difficult journey was the will of Allah.

Soon he came to a pass through the bare, rocky hills. In the distance he saw shady trees and fields. Ya'qub smiled to himself and said the holy words, '*Al-Hamdulillah!*' as he walked towards the settlement.

It was a farming village called Suwadimah, on the outskirts of the city of Faddan. Ya'qub asked the people he met if they knew Laban bin Batwail. They did. He was their Sheikh. One of them pointed to a girl looking after goats nearby.

'That is Rahil, Sheikh Laban's daughter', said the man.

Ya'qub looked towards her and his heart beat faster. She was beautiful. He walked up to her. He tried to hide his feelings, but he found it difficult to speak. He avoided her eyes as he said, 'We don't know each other, although our families are closely connected. I am Ya'qub, the son of Ishaq al-Rasul. My mother is Rifqah, the daughter of your grandmother. I have come across the desert from Kan'an, on a holy journey.'

Rahil kept her head bowed as she greeted him politely and invited him to her father's house.

'This must be the gift of Allah which has been promised to me',

thought Ya'qub, as he followed her along the path. He knew that this girl was to be his wife.

When they arrived at the Sheikh's house, Ya'qub was welcomed warmly. Ya'qub told the Sheikh of Ishaq's request, that Ya'qub should marry one of the Sheikh's daughters and, to his joy, the Sheikh agreed at once. But at the Sheikh's next words, Ya'qub's heart stopped.

'Before you can marry Rahil, there are things you must do', said the Sheikh. 'First you must work here for seven years.'

Ya'qub agreed immediately but the Sheikh had not finished.

'Rahil may not marry before her sister Laiyah', the Sheikh explained.

So Ya'qub married Laiyah first and worked for seven years, then he married Rahil. His household lived in peace and harmony and Ya'qub returned to Kan'an a happy man. He had twelve children. One of them was Yusuf, who was to play an important part in the history of Egypt.